TOP TIPS FOR BRIDES

Copyright © Summersdale Publishers Ltd, 2014

Research by Sarah Herman

Summersdale Publishers Ltd
46 West Street
Chichester
West Sussex
PO19 1RP
UK

www.summersdale.com

Printed and bound in the Czech Republic

ISBN: 978-1-84953-535-9

Substantial discounts on bulk quantities of Summersdale books are available to corporations, professional associations and other organisations. For details contact general enquiries: telephone: +44 (0) 1243 771107, fax: +44 (0) 1243 786300 or email: enquiries@summersdale.com.

W9-BRX-425

TOP TIPS

FOR

BRIDES

Verity Davidson

summersdale

CONTENTS

INTRODUCTION

Congratulations! You're getting married and the big day is fast approaching. As exciting and fun as planning a wedding can be, the hard work involved – combined with the expectations of family and friends, the financial burden and the sheer number of details to remember – can be time-consuming, stressful and nerve-wracking. The wedding day itself, however, should be none of these things. It should be magical, memorable, exhilarating, and a precious collection of wonderful moments, many of which you hadn't even planned on.

You will only be a bride once, so this book brings together experience, common sense and clever fixes to ensure that your special day runs smoothly, remains catastrophe-free and is full of all the highs you could hope for. Read it in advance so you feel calm and collected about what's to come, and refer to it the night before you tie the knot so that on your wedding morning, during the ceremony and even after the last glass of champagne has been drunk, a smile never leaves your face.

THE NIGHT BEFORE

You're getting married in the morning! Ding dong the bells are going to chime! With all the last-minute details to organise and remember, these tips will help make sure chaos and calamity are banished from your wedding eve.

It's OK to have butterflies in your stomach. Just get them to fly in formation.

ROB GILBERT

PREPARING YOURSELF
FOR THE BIG DAY

◇ Make sure you've left the evening before your wedding free to relax and enjoy yourself, either alone or with your friends. No last-minute phone calls to caterers or florists, this way you can start to get excited for your big day without worrying about all the small things.

◇ What you eat and drink the day and night before your wedding should be planned in advance. This is not the time to gorge yourself on chocolate that could cause a break-out, order in a giant pizza that will leave you bloated, or polish off a bottle of wine that could cause a hangover. Stick to light and healthy choices like grilled fish, brown rice, leafy greens – or anything that won't give you a dodgy tummy. And be sure to drink plenty of water for radiant skin.

WINDING DOWN

◇ If you can't face spending the night alone, invite your bridesmaids or best friends round to your house or hotel room for a girly movie evening.

◇ Pamper yourself with a foot spa or manicure, or by painting your nails in preparation for tomorrow.

◇ Read through your wedding vows – it will help to refocus your mind on what the whole day is going to be about.

◇ Cut all the tags off any bridesmaid or flower girl dresses (being sure to remember whose is whose), and make sure all the outfits are steamed.

◇ Try not to call your spouse-to-be; it will make the grand reveal of seeing them the next day all the more special. If you can't resist, send them a special message to tell them how you feel.

DON'T FORGET...

Spend 30 minutes or so going through your wedding checklist of all the items you need for the next day and make sure you know where they're located. Make sure you remember:

- ◇ Dress, skirt and top, or trouser suit

- ◇ Accessories (earrings, necklace, bracelets, rings, etc.)

- ◇ Veil, hairpiece or tiara, clips, grips

- ◇ Shoes (and tights or stockings, if required)

- ◇ Underwear (bra/basque/corset, suspender belt, suspenders, slip/petticoat, garter, knickers/thong, etc.)

◇ Handbag and contents (alternatively, assign the responsibility of your personal items to a close friend or maid of honour)

◇ Coat/bolero

◇ Any other items, e.g. reception dress, alternative dancing shoes, wedding vows, any gifts or personal items you want to bring with you.

Don't worry, just relax…
Enjoy the roses and
breathe them in; enjoy each
moment that you live.

TIFFANY ALVORD

SLEEPING BEAUTY

Getting a good night's sleep before the big day will make sure you look and feel your best when it's time to make your entrance tomorrow. Don't let butterflies get the better of you with these sleep-tastic tips.

◇ Get cosy early in comfy PJs, slippers, and a blanket on the sofa.

◇ Turn the lights down low and sip on a cup of camomile tea or warm milk.

◇ Take a hot bath with essential oils, like lavender or sandalwood.

◇ Listen to calming music, meditate or read a favourite book to send you into a slumber.

◇ If you can, avoid relying on sleeping pills or drinking alcohol – these could affect you negatively the next day.

*You know you're in love
when you can't fall asleep
because reality is finally
better than your dreams.*

DR SEUSS

*Thank God for all I missed,
because it led me here to this.*

Darius Rucker

DISASTER DODGER

Smooth, soft hands are key for avoiding any awkward ring-sticking moments during the ceremony. Treat yourself to a luxury hand cream and prep your digits in time for the big day. Expensive lotions out of your budget? No problem – a homemade remedy of olive oil, lemon juice and a drop of your favourite scented oil will do the trick.

YOUR NOTES

....
....
....
....
....
....
....
....
....
....
....
....
....
....
....
....
....

YOUR NOTES

....
....
....
....
....
....
....
....
....
....
....
....
....
....
....
....

WAKEY-WAKEY!

After months of planning, your big day has finally arrived! Those butterflies might be partying in your stomach, and your home or hotel room may be filled with people, so it's important to relax and make the most of this once-in-a-lifetime experience.

TREATING YOUR ENTOURAGE

Your best friends gave you the royal treatment on your hen-do, so the morning of the wedding is a great chance to reciprocate the love and make sure they look fabulous with professionally applied make-up, hair-dos and manicures.

◇ Bust open the bubbly (not too much, mind!) to calm your nerves and get the party started.

◇ Set the mood with your favourite tunes and reminisce about your hen-do.

◇ If you're having bridesmaids or flower girls, hang all their outfits next to your wedding dress on pretty hangers for a beautiful photo.

When you arise in the morning, think of what a precious privilege it is to be alive – to breathe, to think, to enjoy, to love.

MARCUS AURELIUS

Happily ever after is not a fairy tale. It's a choice.

FAWN WEAVER

DON'T FORGET...

Many brides forget or refuse to eat something on the morning of their wedding. Even if you're feeling nervous it's essential that you make time to sit down (before getting ready) and eat something substantial – it might be later in the day before you have the chance to eat again, and you don't want to faint at the altar. Here are a couple of great wedding breakfast ideas you or your bridesmaids could prepare:

◇ A basket of muffins, chocolate croissants and pastries

◇ Smoked salmon and cream cheese bagels

◇ Fruit salad, yoghurt and granola cups

◇ Bacon sandwiches and scrambled eggs

◇ Don't forget to drink something too, and not just Mimosas!

BOUQUET BEST

◇ As beautiful as your wedding flowers are, they are more likely to stay that way if you handle them as little as possible.

◇ Keep any bouquets nestled in the tissue paper they arrived in, and out of direct sunlight.

◇ Don't put your flowers in the fridge as the sudden change in temperature is likely to do more harm than good.

◇ When you're ready to leave, pluck out any unfortunate-looking petals.

Enjoy the little things in life… For one day you'll look back and realise they were the big things.

KURT VONNEGUT

DISASTER DODGER

The only person who's allowed to be running late today is you! Make sure everyone knows the timetable for having their hair and make-up done, so there are no unexpected delays. Devise realistic time slots with the stylists and beauticians beforehand and pin them up somewhere everyone can see so you don't have to worry about keeping track.

YOUR NOTES

....
....
....
....
....
....
....
....
....
....
....
....
....
....
....

YOUR NOTES

....
....
....
....
....
....
....
....
....
....
....
....
....
....

LOOKING GOOD

There's so much expectation about how the bride looks at a wedding – don't let that faze you. Remember, you will look fabulous. Just relax, smile and let the professionals and your loved ones take over.

FINAL PREPARATIONS

◇ It's lovely to have friends and family come to support you before you head to the venue, but it's a good idea to keep the numbers to a minimum, especially if you're likely to be feeling flustered. Keep anxiety at bay by telling people in advance when is a good time to pop in, if at all, and if you would like them to stay or accompany you to the ceremony.

◇ Appoint someone as your dresser well before the big day. This person should attend your final fitting with you to learn from the sales staff how to correctly fasten your dress. Make sure they wash their hands before helping you and avoid wearing coloured nail polish until your dress has been fastened. Allocate 45 minutes for putting on your dress – this will allow for adjustments, removal of small creases or marks, and lots of time to look in the mirror and make sure you're happy.

STYLE TIPS

◇ In the morning, don't wear a bra
  with straps (especially if your outfit
  is strapless) or socks – red pressure
  marks in your pre-wedding photos
  won't look good.

◇ If possible, you should always step
  into a dress rather than putting it
  over your head, otherwise you could
  ruin your recently styled hair.

◇ Shoes should always be put on last to avoid any damage to your outfit – if you're wearing a voluminous or tight-fitting dress, ask a friendly helper to fasten them for you.

◇ Be careful not to spray perfume onto your wedding dress as it could stain.

◇ Make sure you leave enough time to have a few photographs taken before you leave for the ceremony.

DON'T FORGET...

Your friends and family are there to help, so be sure to let them. You might be nervous and in a panic, so they might be best-placed to help you with the following:

- ◇ Adjusting bra straps

- ◇ Helping you step into your shoes

- ◇ Positioning your veil

- ◇ Painting your nails

- ◇ Straightening your hair

- ◇ Making you a cup of tea

- ◇ Dealing with florists, hair stylists, chauffeurs and any other calls or visitors.

I chose my wife as she did her wedding gown – for qualities that would wear well.

<small>OLIVER GOLDSMITH</small>

*The earth is like a
beautiful bride who needs
no manmade jewels to
heighten her loveliness.*

KAHLIL GIBRAN

HAIR COMES THE BRIDE!

A few pointers to make sure your bridal barnet looks beautiful.

◇ If you're having an up-do, don't wash your hair on the day of the wedding – the natural grease makes it easier for your stylist to create a sculptured look.

◇ Hair stylists generally recommend a consultation for wedding hair a few months before the wedding date, and a trim (if desired) a week or so before.

◇ If you're doing your own hair, give yourself plenty of time to wash, blow-dry, straighten, curl and style – these things can take a lot longer than normal because of all the excitement.

◇ If your stylist can't make it to your location and you have to go to the salon, be sure to factor in contingency time in case of bad traffic, and always take an umbrella even if the sun is shining.

◇ If you change your mind at the last minute about how you want your hair to look, be sure to notify your stylist as soon as possible (preferably before they arrive) so they can bring the appropriate products and equipment for the look you want.

The most beautiful things
in the world cannot be seen
or even touched; they must
be felt with the heart.

DISASTER DODGER

If you want that extra glow to make you feel great and you're planning on slapping on the fake tan, you must plan this into your schedule for the few days leading up to the wedding otherwise there's a good chance your beautiful white dress will end up with tan stains. Use a tried-and-tested product and give it a few days to settle. Check your skin in a mirror under bright daylight (or ask a friend to take a few pictures of you outside) so you can be confident you haven't missed a spot or created any unsightly tan lines.

*The beauty of a woman is
seen in her eyes, because that
is the doorway to her heart,
the place where love resides.*

Audrey Hepburn

YOUR NOTES

....
....
....
....
....
....
....
....
....
....
....
....
....
....
....
....

YOUR NOTES

....
....
....
....
....
....
....
....
....
....
....
....
....
....
....
....

BRIDAL ARRIVAL

*Whatever your mode of transport
or your destination, arriving at
your ceremony venue is a highly
emotional, exciting and important
part of the day. Show up in style
and prepare to make an entrance.*

WORDS OF WISDOM

If your father or another loved one is giving you away, the journey with them to the venue is a special time. They might have some important words of advice to impart to you, but you equally might want to take this time to thank them, tell them how you feel, and perhaps give them a card or gift to show your love and appreciation.

*I love my father as the
stars – he's a bright, shining
example and a happy
twinkling in my heart.*

ADABELLA RADICI

MAKING YOUR ENTRANCE

◇ Even if you're running late, take your time. It's likely you and your partner have waited years for this day, so a few more minutes to feel relaxed won't hurt.

◇ Never walk round the back of a car, always the front – the chance of your beautiful outfit getting caught or damaged on the exhaust is not worth the risk.

◇ If you're being accompanied by a bridal party, ask them to walk in slowly, feel confident and smile. With a large entourage it's a great idea to pair people up so they don't have to walk in solo.

◇ Before you begin your entrance, make sure you're happy with the arm-hold between yourself and your escort so you feel as comfortable as possible.

DON'T FORGET...

Appoint a member of the bridal party responsible for last-minute checks before you enter the ceremony space.

◈ Is your veil or hairpiece sitting OK on your head? Does it need adjusting?

◈ Does the skirt or train fan out neatly and equally around the dress?

◇ If you're wearing a shirt, is the collar neat? Are all the right buttons done up? Are the tails tucked in?

◇ Are there any wisps of hair out of place from the breeze outside?

◇ Have you smudged your make-up? Is there any lipstick on your teeth?

◇ Does your bouquet look its best?

◇ Do the flower girls/pageboys know what they're supposed to do?

◇ Does your maid of honour have your wedding vows (if required) to pass to you?

WALK THE WALK

It's the moment all eyes are on you, and, for some, it's the most nerve-wracking part of the day. Follow these guidelines for a breezy entrance.

◇ Don't zombie-walk your way to the front – look at your guests. The smiles and happy tears of your friends and family will help to relax you.

◇ Hold your bouquet down near your thighs, keeping your arms in a diamond shape for an elegant look, rather than up tight near your chest.

◇ Be sure to look at your father or whoever is walking you down the aisle – remember, this could be a very emotional time for them, too.

◇ Step, together, step, together is a little outdated, but slowing your pace down a tad (especially if you have a short aisle) gives your photographer the chance to get enough pictures of your entrance, and builds the anticipation of being reunited with your fiancé.

DISASTER DODGER

Most brides-to-be have dreamt that horrible nightmare where they trip and face plant while walking down the aisle. Practice makes perfect, but if you don't get the chance, and you're wearing a full-length skirt, ensure a smooth aisle-glide by simply sticking out your foot to take each step and then waiting for the skirt of your dress to come into contact with your ankle before making the next step.

For those opting for short dresses or suits, pace your steps evenly and take your time, this way you can gaze lovingly into your partner's face rather than at the carpet.

Happiness, not in another place but this place... Not for another hour but this hour.

WALT WHITMAN

YOUR NOTES

....
....
....
....
....
....
....
....
....
....
....
....
....
....
....
....
....

YOUR NOTES

....
....
....
....
....
....
....
....
....
....
....
....
....
....
....
....
....
....
....
....

POMP AND CEREMONY

No matter what happens, you will remember this part of the day for the rest of your life: the vows, the music, signing the register, walking down the aisle as a married couple – here's how to do it all with ease.

RESPECTING YOUR VENUE

Weddings are celebratory affairs, but they are also serious matters – both legally and/ or spiritually. Everyone's views differ, but it is often the bride and groom who set the tone for how everyone else behaves. If you're marrying in a place of worship, respect the space you're in and encourage your guests to do the same. If you want a more relaxed approach, it might be advisable to be married in a non-religious setting.

*Marriage is a commitment;
a decision to do, all through
life, that which will express
your love for one's spouse.*

HERMAN H. KIEVAL

KEEPING IT TOGETHER

◇ Look into your fiancé's eyes when you reach the front of your wedding venue – the whole atmosphere will be overwhelming, but the familiarity you share will help calm both your nerves.

◇ If you are doing a reading, remember to take slow, deep breaths, and speak loudly and clearly so all of your guests can enjoy it.

*This done, he took the bride
about the neck; and kiss'd her
lips with such a clamorous
smack, that, at the parting,
all the church did echo.*

WILLIAM SHAKESPEARE

DON'T FORGET...

Kissing for the first time as a married couple can cause problems for some. These following pointers will ensure your smooch goes swimmingly.

◇ No sudden movements – you don't want to butt heads, teeth or noses, so go in nice and slow.

◇ Grab hold of each other and get close – you're married now, so there doesn't need to be a big gap between you.

◇ Keep your eyes closed while you kiss – it will look better in the photos.

◇ Don't practise beforehand – the best kisses are the most natural ones.

◇ Remember where you are and who you're kissing in front of. Be it in a church, in front of your grandmother or the officiant, remember to keep it PG – X-rated kisses are what the honeymoon is for.

VOWS WITH POW

◇ If you are repeating standard vows, make sure you take your time to listen to the words the officiant is saying – these are the promises you're making to your partner, and you want to mean them, rather than robotically regurgitate them.

◇ If you're making additional personal vows, it's a good idea to have them written down – ask a friendly helper to hold on to them and pass the paper to you at the appropriate moment.

◇ Look into each other's eyes, even if you're reading vows.

◇ If your voice starts to waver or you begin to cry, take a second to gather yourself, rather than mumbling through the rest of your vows.

Promise a lot and give even more.

ANTHONY J. D'ANGELO

*Marriage is the golden
ring in a chain whose
beginning is a glance and
whose ending is eternity.*

KAHLIL GIBRAN

DISASTER DODGER

The signing of the register is an important part of the wedding ceremony – officially marking its place in the history books. Make sure there's no awkward confusion by asking friends or relatives in advance if they will sign it for you. This will also prevent anyone being offended on the day for not being asked, causing potential arguments.

YOUR NOTES

....
....
....
....
....
....
....
....
....
....
....
....
....
....
....

YOUR NOTES

....
....
....
....
....
....
....
....
....
....
....
....
....
....
....
....

SAY CHEESE!

*You've gone to all that trouble
to pick out a fabulous location
and look your best, now it's
time to make sure you have the
ultimate keepsake from the day
– a wonderful wedding album
full of fantastic photographs.*

GETTING THE MOST FROM YOUR PHOTOS

◇ Be sure to get any photographs that include your guests out of the way first, so they can get on with enjoying the champagne and canapés while you are whisked off for a snapping session with your photographer.

◇ Make sure a trusted friend or relative is on hand with a pre-discussed list of all the various photograph groupings you would like. Although it's likely you will have discussed these with your photographer beforehand, a list will make sure no friends or relatives are left out.

*There are no bad pictures;
that's just how your face
looks sometimes.*

ABRAHAM LINCOLN

What I like about photographs is that they capture a moment that's gone forever, impossible to reproduce.

LOOKING YOUR BEST

◇ If the weather's feeling cooler, bring a shrug, coat or shawl along to the photography portion of your day to cover up and keep you warm on the small walks between locations.

◇ Smiling for all those photos could leave your jaw a little sore. Make sure you relax your expression after every few photos to avoid face ache and unnatural smiles.

◇ Make sure you're not photographed in direct sunlight – squinting is definitely not your best look.

◇ Don't obsess over how the pictures will turn out – trust your photographer and their experience and enjoy staring lovingly into your other half's eyes.

POSING MASTERCLASS

◇ Standing square to the camera isn't always the best way to show off your outfit. Try turning your body slightly to the side for a more flattering look.

◇ Put all your weight on your back foot, ever so slightly bend the knee of your front leg and point your toe for a beauty-queen finish.

◇ Lift your neck forward to avoid any unwanted chins or creases – this will accentuate the contours of your neck.

◇ Natural smiles are best, so let the photographer make you laugh.

◇ Hold your bouquet down near your thighs, rather than across your stomach for a more informal, relaxed look.

◇ You look amazing, so feel it too and your confidence and joy will shine through in your pictures.

*A photograph can be an
instant of life captured
for eternity that will never
cease looking back at you.*

BRIGITTE BARDOT

DON'T FORGET...

Have the following items to hand while you're having your photos taken:

◇ Hand mirror

◇ Basic make-up touch-up kit

◇ Comb (if your hair requires it – also handy for men with messy hair)

◇ Bobby pins

◇ Battery-operated fan to keep you cool in the sun

◇ A glass of champagne.

May you live as long as you want, may you never want as long as you live.

DISASTER DODGER

With all the excitement, you'll probably be feeling a little flushed. No matter what, take a moment to check your face and apply a little compact powder before your photographs are taken – no one wants a set of sweaty snaps.

The whole point of taking pictures is so that you don't have to explain things with words.

ELLIOTT ERWITT

YOUR NOTES

....

....

....

....

....

....

....

....

....

....

....

....

....

....

....

YOUR NOTES

....
....
....
....
....
....
....
....
....
....
....
....
....
....
....
....
....

A GRAND RECEPTION

The dazzling details of your wedding reception will have caused you no shortage of time and effort – at long last you can enjoy every one of them stress-free. The evening will go by in the blink of a teary eye, so make sure you savour every moment.

MEETING AND GREETING

◇ With all the friends and family around it's easy to spend your entire day chatting with everyone but your other half. Make sure you find each other throughout the night and not just to pose for cameras.

◇ Depending on how many guests are at your wedding, you will have an awful lot of people to meet and greet. Spend more time with your guests at their tables, rather than in a formal receiving line, by starting the dinner first and then greeting people one table at a time between courses. This gives them the opportunity to congratulate you, take your picture and see your outfits up close without the pressure of a moving line.

ENJOYING THE RECEPTION

◇ Sick of carrying your bouquet around all day? Make sure it's displayed for your guests to enjoy it, either on the top table or next to your cake.

◇ Don't leave your guests waiting. Arrive at the venue promptly and make your grand entrance as soon as your guests have arrived – people will be hungry and don't want to wait for hours.

◇ Freshen up your make-up and make any changes to your hair or clothing before entering the reception venue. Once you're there it will be really hard to tear yourself away from friends and family.

*So I commended enjoyment,
because a man has nothing
better under the sun than to
eat, drink and be merry.*

ECCLESIASTES 8:15

*It is not the quantity
of the meat, but the
cheerfulness of the guests,
which makes the feast.*

EDWARD HYDE

DON'T FORGET...

A good wedding planner will make sure all the elements of your wedding come together and are appreciated by your guests. In the absence of one, you might want to check off the following when you arrive at your reception venue:

◇ Have all the decorations/flowers/ furniture you ordered arrived?

◇ Have all the appropriate place cards, party favours and centrepieces been added to the tables?

◇ Is the seating plan positioned where guests can see it?

◇ Have the tables been named or numbered correctly?

◇ Do the guests know the bar policy?

◇ Is there a clear timetable for the staff regarding drinks, food and entertainment?

◇ If you are having any entertainment, has it arrived? Are there any problems?

◇ What is the schedule for any musical elements to the reception?

DINNER DOS AND DON'TS

Eating at a wedding is all about enjoying yourself and tucking into whatever you fancy. Forget about the pre-wedding diet, relax and make the most of it.

◇ This is your wedding and you're paying for all this amazing food, so even if you're in a tight-fitting dress or if the excitement has zapped your appetite, do try to eat something, especially if you're drinking alcohol.

◇ Eat gracefully with a large napkin across your lap – there'll be no hiding any giant food stains on your white dress or perfectly pressed trouser suit.

◇ Save room for cake! Your cake is never going to taste as good as on your wedding day. If you're a dessert person, this might be something you spent hours picking out so make sure you're not too stuffed to enjoy some!

◇ Follow each glass of alcohol with a full glass of water to stay hydrated and to ward off the more unglamorous effects of drinking.

I dreamed of a wedding of elaborate elegance; a church filled with flowers and friends. I asked him what kind of wedding he wished for; he said one that would make me his wife.

ANONYMOUS

DISASTER DODGER

More and more couples are choosing outside wedding reception venues, which can be magical and make for great photos. What doesn't look so great, however, is sunburn. Make sure you've brought a high-factor sunscreen with you to the venue. Apply it on arrival (or in the morning if your ceremony is also outside) and make sure you reapply throughout the day, otherwise you'll be Photoshopping red blotches out of your wedding album.

Cherish your human connections – your relationships with friends and family.

BARBARA BUSH

YOUR NOTES

....
....
....
....
....
....
....
....
....
....
....
....
....
....
....

YOUR NOTES

....
....
....
....
....
....
....
....
....
....
....
....
....
....
....
....

TOASTS AND CAKE

*You survived the walk down
the aisle, the first kiss, the grand
entrance – but now comes the real
test: the speeches. Soak up the love
and pride of your guests and the
sweetness of your cake, and be
prepared for the occasional cringe!*

A BIT OF
BUBBLY

Newsflash: not everyone likes drinking champagne! Avoid half-drunk glasses of the pricey pop being poured away after the toasts by asking your bartender to only pour out a few bottles. Ask guests to collect a glass from the bar if they so choose, or refresh their current drink. Depending on the length of your guest list, you could save a small fortune!

*Let us celebrate the occasion
with wine and sweet words.*

PLAUTUS

KEEPING THE TOASTS
IN CHECK

◇ Make sure your DJ or toastmaster knows who's speaking and in what order to keep the evening moving. If your husband's best man or one of his friends is running things, keep an eye on how much they're drinking during dinner to avoid the toasts turning into a second stag night.

◇ Have those people giving the speeches stand beside the cake table – it makes for a lovely backdrop for photographs, and means that the whole room can be addressed, including those at the top table.

◇ It's a good idea to keep speeches to a minimum, and a time limit, otherwise guests can become restless. Or break speeches up with dinner courses, music, entertainment or a slideshow of photographs.

◇ Cut your cake and throw the bouquet immediately after the speeches when you have everyone's attention and all your guests are still present.

THE FIRST DANCE

◇ If you're having a first dance, wait until your caterer has cut up the wedding cake and served it to your guests, that way they have something to nibble on while you're strutting your stuff.

◇ Don't fancy having your dancing skills on display? Avoid the first dance by inviting everyone onto the dance floor immediately after the cutting of the cake.

I was the best man at a wedding one time… If I'm the best man, why is she marrying him?

JERRY SEINFELD

DON'T FORGET...

It's traditional for the groom to say a few words, but don't feel that you have to keep tight-lipped. Either way, make sure one of you remembers to thank the following people:

◇ Both sets of parents, especially those who contributed to the cost of the wedding

◇ The maid of honour, best man, bridesmaids and groomsmen, and give them any token gifts you have bought

◇ Any flower girls or pageboys

◇ Your families for welcoming you both and for coming to the wedding

◇ Any other friends or family who have contributed significantly to the wedding (e.g. making the cake, doing the flowers, etc.).

OH CRUMBS!

Cake traditions you might want to incorporate include:

◇ Gift-wrap pieces of wedding cake for unmarried friends (superstition says that if they sleep with it under their pillow, they will dream of their future spouse that night).

◇ Feeding cake to each other isn't just a fun way to cover your spouse's face in buttercream – it's a symbol of your promise to provide for each other for the rest of your lives.

◇ Saving the top tier or part of your cake for your first anniversary or even the celebration of your first baby. To do this, wrap it in several layers of cling film and a layer of foil, and place in an airtight bag or box (remember to label it so you don't forget to enjoy it next year!). Fruit cakes and most sponges should last frozen for six months to a year – some commercial cakes with preservatives can last even longer in the freezer – but check with your baker first.

In all of the wedding cake,
hope is the sweetest of plums.

Douglas Jerrold

Cakes are special… Every celebration ends with something sweet, a cake, and people remember. It's all about the memories.

BUDDY VALASTRO

DISASTER DODGER

Make sure you've checked with your baker how best to cut the cake. Tiered cakes usually contain dowels and plates, which are required to maintain the structure. Cutting around these rather than into them will prevent any cake catastrophes. The caterers at your venue can then take over and serve the cake to your guests.

YOUR NOTES

....
....
....
....
....
....
....
....
....
....
....
....
....
....
....
....

YOUR NOTES

....
....
....
....
....
....
....
....
....
....
....
....
....
....
....
....

PARTY TIME

Toasts and treats done, it's time to gossip, gulp and gyrate the night away with friends and family, and – most importantly – your shiny new husband!

MAKING YOUR EXIT

You don't want to be one of the last people on the tiles, but equally you don't want to miss out on the party you're paying for. Have your mode of transportation ready to pick you up about an hour before the planned end of your reception. Then you have the option to have a proper send-off with all your guests before they leave, or stay a little longer if the party is going strong.

*Opportunity dances
with those already on
the dance floor.*

H. JACKSON BROWN JR

*Dancing is the poetry
of the foot.*

JOHN DRYDEN

SHARING THE LOAD

No matter how much hard work you put into planning your wedding, you don't want to be left doing all the heavy lifting at the end of the night. Arrange for family members or friends to take charge of transporting any wedding gifts, centrepieces and leftover wedding cake, so you can head to your post-nuptial love nest worry-free.

THE LIFE OF THE PARTY

◇ Slip into some more comfortable shoes or a smaller dress if you want to party hard.

◇ If you have extra guests arriving just for the evening, make sure you go out of your way to greet them and socialise with them on the dance floor.

◇ If the DJ isn't playing the music you agreed on, or you think your guests would appreciate something different, don't be afraid to ask – it's your party!

◇ Ask your best friends to invite shy relatives and single friends onto the dance floor so no one feels left out.

◇ Golden oldies and dorky dance moves may seem cheesy, but they'll get everyone on their feet feeling comfortable and having fun.

DON'T FORGET...

As much as you might love a good party, not everyone's a dancer – here are some great ways to make sure everyone has a good time!

◇ Have a quieter room or area away from the dance floor where people can talk to each other without shouting.

◇ Spend a bit more time earlier in the evening with elderly relatives or non-dancing types so you don't feel guilty running off to boogie later on.

◇ Make sure there are some late-night snacks if you're expecting people to party well into the night – a selection of savoury snacks such as sandwiches, pies, burgers, chicken wings or chips is a good idea. Don't forget to provide some late-night options for anyone with special dietary needs.

◇ Ask the DJ to alternate the tempo of the music so there are slow dances and chances for people to hydrate and take a break.

*Music expresses that
which cannot be put into
words and that which
cannot remain silent.*

VICTOR HUGO

If music be the food of love, play on.

WILLIAM SHAKESPEARE

DISASTER
DODGER

If there are a number of children attending your wedding, it's a good idea to start the dance proceedings with more kid-friendly songs (or even allocate a separate space in the venue for a kids' party). This way they'll tire themselves out early and avoid being accidental victims of a crowded dance floor later in the night.

YOUR NOTES

....
....
....
....
....
....
....
....
....
....
....
....
....
....
....
....

YOUR NOTES

....
....
....
....
....
....
....
....
....
....
....
....
....
....
....
....

HONEYMOONERS

Your wedding was the day of your dreams, and now it's all over you might feel a little deflated. These tips will make sure you keep that bridal blush long after the last dance of the night.

LIFE GOES ON

◇ For some couples who already live together, own a house, have children and share bank accounts, not much will change after the wedding is over, but it's still important to make time to celebrate this exciting transition in your lives as a couple. Organise a dinner party with close friends, book your honeymoon or a weekend away and start making plans for your home and your future.

◇ Boring as it may seem after wedding outfits, accessories and decorations, you might want to start thinking about your financial situation: bank accounts, life insurance, pensions and your savings. You also might want to write a will (if you already have individual wills these should be rewritten now you're married). These might be things you've avoided before but there's no time like the present to cement yourself as a married couple.

SHORT TIPS

◇ Don't panic if you don't have sex on your wedding night – it's quite common to pass out after such a long day and all that partying. It doesn't mean you love each other any less, and remember: there's always the morning after and the rest of your lives for the good stuff.

◇ If you're not leaving for a honeymoon immediately, enjoy a few days together relaxing, taking long walks and steamy showers and avoid feeling the post-wedding blues by reminiscing about the big day and opening your gifts.

◇ Create an invite-only file-sharing depository online using a site like Flickr or Dropbox for all your nearest and dearest to upload and share any pictures they took.

◇ If you have a wedding website, send out a general message to everyone thanking them for coming.

Chains do not hold a marriage together. It is threads, hundreds of tiny threads, which sew people together through the years.

SIMONE SIGNORET

*A happy marriage is a
long conversation which
always seems too short.*

ANDRÉ MAUROIS

DON'T FORGET...

The wedding may be over, but there could still be a few things to tick off your to-do list:

⬥ Paying any invoices for wedding goods and services

⬥ Having your wedding outfits dry-cleaned

◇ Changing your name, if you have chosen to, with all the relevant organisations (banks, credit card companies, doctors, the tax office, your driver's licence and passport)

◇ Packing for the honeymoon

◇ Chasing up the photographer and/or videographer for the pictures and video from the wedding.

HOW TO HONEYMOON

◇ Don't put too much pressure on the honeymoon to be the most amazing time of your lives. Chances are it will be fantastic, but too much pressure for lots of sex, exceptional hotels and perfect weather can cause disappointment.

◇ Book a special activity in advance to surprise your husband (e.g. scuba-diving lessons or a helicopter ride).

◇ It's healthy to spend a bit of the honeymoon apart to reflect on the wedding and the future. A stroll along the beach, a yoga class or a massage by yourself will give you both the necessary space to truly unwind and enjoy the trip.

◇ Mention you're on your honeymoon everywhere you go – you never know what freebies are on offer to lovebirds.

*He's more myself than I am.
Whatever our souls are made
of, his and mine are the same.*

Emily Brontë

DISASTER DODGER

When the confetti settles, you're left with all those wonderful memories and possibly a large collection of gifts. Don't forget to keep cards and gift tags with their respective pressies until you've had time to draw up a list and write your thank-you notes (which you should aim to do within a couple of weeks of the wedding). A good rule is to not use a gift or spend a voucher until you have expressed your gratitude.

YOUR NOTES

YOUR NOTES

....
....
....
....
....
....
....
....
....
....
....
....
....
....

If you're interested in finding out more about our books, find us on Facebook at **Summersdale Publishers** and follow us on Twitter at **@Summersdale**.

www.summersdale.com